The heart of Christmas

By Michael Jobling

The Heart of Christmas

ISBN 978-0-9565818-0-8

Printed and bound by www.lulu.com

Published in Great Britain by
Treasure House Creative, Milton Keynes

Introduction

Behind the Christmas tree, beyond Father Christmas, wrapped in the tinsel and trimmings, more nourishing than the turkey, more surprising than what's in the crackers, more delightful than the tree lights, is the reality at the heart of Christmas. Not a fairy-tale but a real event that happened to real people in a real place and changed history.

These cameo word sketches and meditations aim to help you to get to the heart of Christmas by looking through the eyes of those it happened to. It builds a bridge between their experience and ours – one we can cross to draw near to the manger ourselves.

This book is the result of half a lifetime of research and reflection. I've tried to be accurate with historical facts and faithful to scripture but I've also prayerfully made use of my imagination, and some clues in the Bible, to bring people to life. They may not all have been exactly as I describe but, hopefully, I'm not too far off the mark. Where I've quoted the New Testament, I have gone to the original Greek and translated it myself.

I hope you enjoy it. You might want to devour it in one go, or just thumb through and read bits that draw your attention. To get the best out of it, I suggest you read one chapter a day to help you prepare for Christmas. If you start on December 13 (my birthday!) you'll finish it on Christmas Day.

Alternatively, if someone has given you this book as a Christmas present (there's a good idea!) you can start on Boxing Day and finish on 6 January (twelfth night) which is traditionally the end of the Christmas festival in the Western church and the day when Orthodox Christians celebrate their Christmas Day.

Either way, I hope this book will transform your Christmas and make it special.

Mike Jobling

Contents

DAY ONE

Dumbstruck!

(Zachariah)

Zachariah didn't like change. He liked things to stay the same. He hadn't always been that way. There was a time, when he was younger, that he had been ambitious and sure of himself – full of the latest ideas and wanting to change everything.

In those days he had wanted to bring things up to date, to try new ideas. In those days his conversation had always been about the future: what he was going to do next week, next year, when he had the money – hopes for this and plans for that.

But those days were gone now. The change had been gradual – so slow that no-one noticed. He was still talkative but now it was all in the past tense:

"Do you remember when we …"

"I remember when old so and so …"

"There used to be a …"

"Have I ever told you about the day I …"

… and so on.

He would sit for hours in the village square talking endlessly about his memories to anyone who would listen. Now, rather than trying to change things, he tried to keep them as they were – his dinner on the table at the same time every day, his daily walk to the village and back at the same time every morning, everything in the same place and time. He got annoyed if things were altered.

Zachariah was semi-retired now, but he still had a spare-time role as a priest. There were too many descendants of Levi for all of them to be occupied in the temple full time, so they served on a rota basis. Once in a while Zachariah's turn for temple duty came round, and he would make the journey to Jerusalem. He would stay there for a few weeks in one of the rooms at the temple and perform any one of a number of tasks which were distributed by lot.

He grumbled when his turn came round, but in some ways it was still part of his settled routine. The temple was like a second home. He knew his way around, he knew what was expected of him. He was on first name terms with the High Priest and he enjoyed meeting old friends from around the country, regaling them with his fund of stories that all began: "I remember when …"

Zachariah missed Elisabeth while he was at the temple,

THE JEWISH PRIESTHOOD

There were around 7,200 priests at the time of Jesus. All the priests traced their ancestry back to Levi, the son of Aaron, the brother of Moses. They were divided into 24 "courses", each of which did service in Jerusalem for one week in turn, from Sabbath to Sabbath. In between times, each of them pursued an ordinary trade or profession. King Herod arranged for many priests to be trained as carpenters and stonemasons to help build a new temple which was still under construction in Zechariah's day, and indeed throughout the lifetime of Jesus.

and couldn't wait to get back home to her. The couple had been together for almost forty years. Their relationship had been through some stormy patches but now it was secure and comfortable. Sometimes Elisabeth had blamed him, and then he had blamed her. But they'd stuck it out, learned a lot and grown comfortable with each other. Their one big regret was that God hadn't granted them any children. They had prayed and prayed, but to no avail. God didn't see fit to answer. Eventually they stopped hoping because they were too old, but it still hurt.

The one thing that never changed with Zachariah, all through his life, was his inability to be silent. He was a chatterbox as a boy, garrulous as a young man. Now, when there was no-one else present to listen to his long-winded stories, he had developed the habit of muttering to himself under his breath. Today, he'd drawn the incense duty. He stood outside the temple, facing a crowd of people who had gathered to pray. He recited the familiar words, waved the incense burner around and then shuffled off into the holy part of the temple, muttering to himself as he went. He hardly had to think about what he was doing or where he was going – he had done it so many times before. "Here we are then … it's a bit dark in here … watch your step old son … don't trip over …" he went straight from his muttering into the familiar words of the prayer he had recited many times before.

Then something caught his eye, and he stopped in his tracks, the prayer incomplete. Someone was standing by the altar of incense, on the far side, looking at him through the smoke. His body jerked with surprise. His heart stopped for a second and then started to beat like a soldier's drum. Someone stood there, dressed in clothes that seemed to glow from within with a white light so painful, his eyes couldn't bear to look.

"Don't be scared, Zachariah,". the figure said, gently, and then it launched into a declaration in poetic form in a voice that seemed to shake the walls with its authority:

> "Your prayer has been heard.
> Your wife, Elisabeth is going to bear you a son
> and you are to name him John.
> He will be a joy and delight
> and many people will rejoice at his birth,
> for he will be great before the Lord.
> He must drink no wine or strong drink –
> he will be filled with the Holy Spirit from his mother's belly.
> He will turn many of the descendants of
> Israel back to the Lord their God.
> This child will go ahead of Him
> in the Spirit and power of Elijah,
> to make fathers consider their children
> and the disobedient return to right ways of thinking.
> He is going to organise a community of
> people who are ready for the Lord's coming."

Zachariah regained his composure and tried to work out whether this was a hoax or a religious experience. Whichever, he decided his best plan was to play along and see what happened.

"That's all very well, sir" he answered, "but how can I be sure you're not having me on? I'm an old man now and my wife is getting on as well; we certainly asked for children – several years ago. We would have welcomed them then, but it's a bit difficult now … "

"I – am – Gabriel," the person replied, with more than a hint of irritation. "I represent God and I have been sent to announce these things. Now look: since you would not believe what I said (which *will* happen – *exactly* at the right time) you are going to be unable to speak. Until it happens."

REJOICE O BARREN WOMAN!

Several other women in the Bible had difficulty bearing children. All but one eventually conceived.

Sarah, Abraham's wife, was the first. God promised Abram that he would have a son and that all the nations of the earth would be blessed through his seed. In spite of this promise, Sara remained barren. Eventually, she encouraged Abraham to have sex with her slave girl. The slave girl, Hagar, became pregnant and bore Abraham a son, Ishmael, but then Hagar began to show disrespect for Sara, and conflict took place in the family as a result. Eventually, Sara bore Abraham a son when he was a hundred years old.
(See Genesis 16 v. 21)

Rachel had children but was not as fertile as her sister Leah, who was also married to Jacob. She suffered pangs of jealousy and disappointment as a result. (See Genesis 30)

Samson's parents had difficulty conceiving and Samson was born to them in response to God's promise. (see Judges 13).

Hannah was married to a man who also had another wife. While her rival, Peninah, had no trouble producing babies, Hannah remained barren until she went to the place of worship, pleaded with God, and then gave birth to Samuel. (See 1 Samuel 1 & 2)

Although these women had difficulty in conceiving, every one eventually did become pregnant and in each case, their child was significant in God's purposes.

The City of Jerusalem, after all its inhabitants had been taken away into exile by the Babylonians, was likened to a barren woman (See Isaiah 54).

The only barren woman in the bible who remained barren was **Michal**, David's first wife. She despised him for making an exhibition of himself as he danced before the ark of the covenant as it was brought into Jerusalem. The Bible says she never bore a child.
(See 2 Samuel 6).

For nine months, not another word passed Zachariah's lips.

The waiting crowd saw him emerge from behind the curtain, making all kinds of gestures in an attempt to communicate what he had seen. He stayed on in the temple until the end of the week, going about his duties in total silence, and then he went home.

Elisabeth was astounded at the information he scribbled on a writing board. Without being able to talk he had to find other ways to tell her how pleased he was to be home. It was nice being kissed and hugged and caressed instead of being talked at incessantly. That night they made love and within a few days, Elisabeth knew something amazing was happening to her.

Now it was her turn to be talkative. Because of her age, everyone agreed she should stay at home and rest and not do anything energetic but everyone in the village wanted to come and see her. She talked endlessly about babies and birth and breastfeeding and how sick she was in the mornings. She described every kick and movement she could feel as the baby began to move and she went on and on about how good God was and how she didn't feel disgraced any more. And Zachariah listened.

In silence.

Elisabeth went to the full term of her pregnancy and gave birth to a son. The neighbours and her family got together and held an enormous party to celebrate. And when the baby was eight days old the whole village gathered to witness the circumcision and naming ceremony. The guests gathered and Zachariah greeted each one in silence – with a nod, a raised eyebrow, or a kiss on both cheeks, as the relationship demanded.

"What is the name of this child?" asked the *mohel* (the official who performed the circumcision).

"He's called John." Elisabeth replied.

A mumur of disapproval ran through the crowd of relatives.
"She can't call him John."
"There's nobody called John in our family."
"Who's John when he's at home?"
"She should name him after her father."
"I thought they'd name him after Zachariah's brother."

Zachariah's brother stepped in.

"Look, Elisabeth, I don't know where you got this crazy idea, but I'm not going to stand by and see my brother humiliated like this. Now, Zachariah, it's your job to name the child. What are you going to call him?"

Zachariah made signs as if writing on something. Someone fetched him a slate and a pencil.

His tongue sticking out of the side of his mouth, he wrote carefully and deliberately. The pencil squeaked as he scratched away. Finally he showed his brother what he had written:

"His name is John."

Zachariah held it up for all to see.

"His name is John" he said, firmly, and then:

"Oh!" ***"Oho!"***

"His name is John. His name is John. His name is John. That's what the angel told me to call him. You see, that's why I haven't been able to talk all this while. I was doing incense duty in the temple and I got to the altar and ..."

... and the whole story came spilling out, along with all his thoughts and feelings for the previous ten months. It was a while before they could shut him up and get on with the ceremony.

Which goes to show that God has a sense of humour, and a sense of timing, and does answer prayer, even if it isn't always in our timescale.

And Zachariah's story also reminds us that, if we were prepared to talk less and listen more, we might find ourselves more in tune with what God is doing.

Prayer

Lord, I ask for your mercy for those whose voice has been silenced, whether by illness, by circumstance, by ridicule or political pressure from those in power. Please raise up people to speak on their behalf.

Please open my ears to you and to others and help me to be a good listener.

You can read the story of Zachariah and Elisabeth in the Bible in Luke, chapter 1.

DAY TWO

Awesome!

(Mary)

Mariam stood at the back of the room, her dark eyes sparkling as she laughed. It was funny watching Zachariah's face as he discovered he could talk again. Zachariah and Elisabeth held a special place in her affections and she was so happy for them.

Mariam was Elisabeth's cousin, but the age difference was so great, she was more like a niece. In some ways Zachariah and Elisabeth were like a second Mum and Dad to her. Unable to have children themselves, they had compensated by making Mariam welcome in their home. She often came to visit and she had been over the moon when they invited her to stay so she and Elisabeth could help each other through their pregnancies.

In a few months, Mariam would be holding her own baby in her arms. The last few months had brought the two women even closer as they shared similar experiences – Elisabeth inexplicably pregnant for the first time in her late fifties, Mariam inexplicably pregnant for the first time as a teenage virgin – and both conceptions accompanied by a visit from an angel! Both women had been the butt of gossip. An experience which each would have found difficult alone was made easier by the strength they gained from each other.

Mariam remembered how excited they had been when she first arrived to see Elisabeth after they both found they were pregnant. Elisabeth said she felt her baby jump up and down inside her when Mariam walked through the door. They had ended up dancing round the room for joy and Mariam had broken into song. There was nothing unusual in that – she was always singing. It was the power of the words that suddenly came onto her lips that surprised her. She'd written them down later, so she didn't forget them:

> "He has shown strength with His arm
> He has scattered those who think in an arrogant way
> He has dragged the powerful from their thrones
> And lifted everyday people to places of influence
> He has filled the hungry with good things
> And sent the rich away with empty hands
> He has remembered his mercy
> And helped his servant Israel
> As he promised our fathers
> 'To Abraham and His seed forever'."

Where had those words come from? What did they mean? Something was happening which was big and important, something that would shape the future of of the nation – maybe of the whole human race – and her baby was part of it! It made her feel small, vulnerable and yet excited, and incredibly alive. And she still couldn't understand: why her? She was just an ordinary girl from an insignificant, north country town. There were hundreds of Mariams in Galilee and Judah. Why her?

It all started with the angel.

She guessed it was an angel, though it didn't exactly say, "Hello, I'm an angel." In fact it had been more abrupt and matter of fact than she would have expected an angel to be. One morning, she

MARY

Mary is an abbreviation of the Latin name Maria. This in turn was an abbreviation of a Greek name, Mariam (the New Testament was written in Greek). However, if Mary and her family spoke the native Aramaic that ordinary people in Galilee spoke, they would have called her Mariamne (pronounced "Marry am knee"). This in turn started out as a Hebrew name, Miriam. The first Miriam in Jewish history was the sister of Moses. She watched over the basket in the bulrushes and later led the children of Israel in a dance of joy after they passed through the Red Sea. Mariamne was a popular name at the and of the fhe 1st century BC, not only because of Moses' sister but also because it was the name of King Herod's Queen. There were hundreds of Mariamnes in Judea at the time of Jesus' birth. The most important thing about Mary was that she was ordinary. God chose an ordinary young woman, from an ordinary family for the special task of being the mother of the Messiah.

was standing in the house and, all of a sudden, there it was, talking to her:

"Hi there, lady blessed by God – the Lord is with you."

To begin with she hadn't even been startled – funny, that. She didn't shout "Oh, God, it's an angel!", or scream. She just thought: "this is weird!", and then she thought: "What kind of a greeting is that?" It was the first time she had been called a lady, rather than a girl, let alone "blessed by God" – and people usually said "the Lord *be* with you", not "the Lord *is* with you".

Then, it suddenly hit her: this isn't just "weird"; it's "awesome"! She had begun to shake and panic. Not for long though: the angel began to speak so gently and kindly, she found herself thinking "Isn't he sweet!"

"Don't be frightened, Mariam. You have found favour with God. Watch what's going to happen. You are going to become pregnant and bear a child, and you are to name him Jeshuah. He will be great and will be called son of the Most High. The Lord is going to give Him the throne of his ancestor, David. He will reign over Jacob's family for ever. His kingdom is never going to come to an end."

"What kind of a girl does he think I am?" She had thought. Maybe he's got the wrong address or something? That message couldn't be for her. Then she spoke:

"Well, you see, I don't want to be awkward but, are you sure you've got the right person. You see, I haven't had sex with a man yet, and I don't intend to until I'm married, so . . . how could I become pregnant?" There was a slight hint of annoyance in her voice. Just a slight hint. The angel's reply had more than a hint of annoyance in it, though.

"The Holy Spirit is going to be released on you, and you will be overshadowed by the power of the Most High. For this reason, the child born to you will be called the Holy Son of God. See, your cousin Elisabeth has conceived a son in her old age, even though they had pronounced her barren. She's in her sixth month now. Nothing is impossible with God."

The angel stood, silent, looking at her as if he was expecting a reply.

What could she say? Did she have a choice? She didn't dare ask. You don't say "no" to a messenger from God. A thousand scary questions raced through her mind in a second: how would she explain it to Mum and Dad? How would they tell Joseph? What would people in the village say when she started to show? Could this be a dream? If so, what did it mean? Was she going mad?

What would it be like to be a king's mother? Would she have morning sickness? Would the "power of the Most High" hurt?

In the end, she spoke:

"Well, yes. OK. I'm the Lord's slave girl. Let it happen – what you said."

And then the angel disappeared. As it did she experienced a totally new sensation, a mixture of intense joy and inner warmth that made her body feel relaxed and heavy and kind of fluttery inside. It lasted for a while and then she rubbed her eyes and thought:

"That didn't happen. I must be imagining things."

She got on with her chores, singing as she did so. She put the strange experience out of her mind and thought nothing more of it – until she missed her period.

She didn't have a choice; and yet she did. She could have said "No! No way! Not me! Choose somebody else." But in a moment of abandonment to God, she simply said "Let it be". If she had said "No!", it would not have stopped the incarnation. God would have chosen one of the hundreds of other Mariams who lived in Israel at the time – or someone with a different name. Maybe the leading roles in all the school nativity plays would have been Simeon and Rebecca or Benjamin and Salome, but Jesus would still have been born. He might have been a fisherman's son, a farmer's son or a baker's son, but he would still have been nailed to the cross.

Mary's "OK" was a big one. She might not have said it at all, if she had known where it would lead: bringing up a son who always knew better than you and was always right; having to wait for him to see to everyone else before she could talk to him and then for him to be so tired, she felt guilty for bothering him. If she had known what it would be like to watch her baby flogged and lynched and nailed to a cross; if she had known what it would be like to be like a mother to his disciples, to love them for his sake and then see most of them crucified or stoned to death, one after another …

It was a big "OK", but she said it. Her "OK" set a pattern to follow. Saying "OK" to God is the essence of being a disciple.

It doesn't matter how ordinary you are, how poor, how young, how insignificant in the eyes of other people. a simple "yes" to God can make you special. Miracles happen when ordinary people say "yes" to God. God doesn't look for people who have already made it and have everything. He looks for people who are willing to be made into something and hungry to have what He can give. People like Mary – people, perhaps, like you.

As Paul wrote to the Corinthian Christians:

> "Look at your call, brothers and sisters – not many of you are naturally wise, not many are powerful, not many of you were born into influential families. But God has chosen the ridiculous things of this world to embarrass the strong, and He has chosen the low things of the world, the despised things, the things that are nothing, to destroy the things that are something, so that no beings of flesh and blood will have reason to boast in His presence."
>
> – I Corinthians 1 v 26–29

Somewhere, in the boredom or chaos of this day, God is going to present you with a possibility. A dream for the future. It may be big or it may be small. But you will have a choice.

You can say,

“No way! not me!”,

or you can say,

“Let it be”.

Your “let it be” could bring Jesus’ presence into part of this world. A new Christmas, with you in a leading role, but Him at the centre.

Prayer

Lord, help me to know when you are opening the door for me - and give me the courage to step through. Let my response to you always be a joyful. “yes!”

You can read the story of Mary and the angel in the Bible in Luke, chapter 1.

DAY THREE

Meticulous

(Joseph)

Joseph was the kind of person who liked things done properly. I can just imagine him saying: "there's a right way of doing everything." He liked things in order. I can picture him, at the end of each day, arranging his tools neatly in the rack in his carpenter's shop and sweeping the shavings from the floor so everything was tidy and clean, ready for the next day's work. Joseph was the kind of man who liked everything to be exactly right and wouldn't rest until he had achieved it. I dare say some people found him inflexible and fussy but the furniture he made was solid and his workmanship was second to none.

I've met a few men like Joseph: engineers, accountants, architects and a warehouse manager among them. They had a lot in common with each other and Joseph would have been happy in their company. These were men who could make measurements accurate to several decimal places and balance the books to a penny. Men who understood attention to detail.

They could make wonderful machinery, build solid houses and could be trusted with money. But sometimes, in their attention to detail, they missed the big picture: what the machinery was for, who lived in the houses and what the funds were financing. They were men who pursued their lives with careful logic and great attention to detail, but were suspicious of the emotional side of life. Perhaps you know someone like that? Maybe you're like that yourself – in that case you'll understand Joseph very well.

Joseph's approach to marriage was as thorough and careful as his carpentry. He had seen other men rush into it, some as a result of their lack of self control, some in response to pressure from their family. But not Joseph. He didn't trust passion and romance. He was determined to go about it the right, way. He would wait until he could afford to keep a wife and then choose wisely, with his head, rather than his heart.

The day eventually came when his financial position was secure and then he chose a wife. He picked an intelligent, fit, healthy and godly young woman from a good family. He spoke to Mariam's father and made the agreement to marry her. The woman didn't have a lot of say in those days and, since Joseph was such an upstanding, kind and prosperous man, her parents would not hear a word against the match. After the appropriate lapse of time Joseph and Mariam, or Mary, were betrothed.

A year after the betrothal, the wedding was due to take place. When the time came

NO ROOM AT THE INN

The phrase "no room at the inn" conjures up a picture of a "no vacancies" sign in the window of an English pub, with the stable as a shed at the back.

In fact the "inn" would have been a large, two-story building, built round a central courtyard with a well in the middle where animals could be watered. Round the courtyard at ground level were alcoves where guests could stable their animals. Stairways led to a first floor terrace, off which were rooms where travellers could bed down for the night.

When Mary and Joseph arrived, all the first floor rooms were occupied, so they had no alternative but to sleep among the animals below. The other occupants of the stable would have been camels and mules or horses, rather than cattle.

Joseph would collect his bride and take her home. This would be the occasion for a huge celebration. Joseph was making meticulous plans for the wedding party. Arrangements for the feast were running smoothly. Then something happened that changed Joseph forever.

"Pregnant?"

Joseph struggled to take in what Mariam was saying. His heart pounded and his whole body trembled with shock. His carefully crafted, painstakingly constructed life was falling apart.

If Mariam had confessed to a love affair with another man, he could understand, though it would be bad enough. But all this talk of angels appearing...! Mariam had to be lying, and yet it was so out of character. And what did one do in a situation like this? He prided himself on doing everything the right way – what was the right way to handle this situation?

His first instinct was to expose Mary to public shame and demand compensation from her family. But was that the *right* thing to do? Ihe more he considered it, the more it seemed wrong. It was just and appropriate, but at the same time it was cruel, selfish and unmerciful.

No. He would just put Mary away quietly – terminate the marriage, but not make a big fuss about it. That would be kind as well as just. So, Matthew tells us, "being a righteous man (righteous = always behaving in the right way) he decided to dismiss her quietly."

True righteousness always combines justice and mercy. There is a spurious righteousness that was around in Joseph's time and is still common today. Ihe Pharisees displayed it then and today it often motivates the tabloid press. It is driven by the desire to expose people who do wrong and to make them pay for the damage they do. But it contrasts with God's righteousness which is motivated by love for both victim and criminal, along with hatred of the sin. Pharisees always demand exposure of the facts: name names! Root out the truth! Expose the culprits!' But that's not God's way. There's a place for just desserts and reaping what you've sown, but that's for God to decide, not us. If Mary had done wrong, God would see she was punished. Joseph didn't need to do it for Him. He chose true righteousness by his decision to put her away quietly, and leave her in God's hands.

We can learn from Joseph – to temper justice with mercy, to allow dignity to the abuser as well as the victim, to consider the criminal's relatives as well as the criminal, to be compassionate, even when we are administering punishment, and to work for restoration and reconciliation, rather than retribution. Like Joseph, we can choose to do the *really* right thing.

At least, he was going to, the next morning, but by the time he had made up his mind it was late and he had to sleep on it.

While he slept, he dreamed.

If Joseph had seen an angel while he was awake he would have convinced himself it couldn't possibly have been real and would probably have ignored it. But while he was asleep, his guard was down. Even so, it was a shock to the system for such a well-regulated man.

"Joseph, descendant of David," said the angel, "don't be afraid to take Mary as your wife, for what has been conceived in her is from the Holy Spirit. She will give birth to a son and he will be called Jeshuah ('Jahweh rescues'), because he is going to rescue his people from their wrongdoing."

The dream had an impact on him. For the first time in his well-ordered life Joseph did something reckless – something that was risky and (in the eyes of the rest of the community) improper. He decided to married a woman who was already pregnant by someone else.

After that, Joseph never quite got control of his life again. However hard he tried to bring things to order, nothing would stay as he wanted it to be. He started making plans for the baby. A carpenter would surely have made a cradle for his first child. A craftsman like Joseph would have made toys, decorated a room for the baby – built a whole new house for the family even. But the census came, and they had to travel to Bethlehem. He planned to stay in the village inn but there wasn't room and Mary's son was born in a stable. Luke refers to Mary as Joseph's "betrothed", implying that the wedding ceremony had not yet taken place. Joseph must have felt resentful – all his plans were going astray, things weren't happening how they should and there was his adopted son lying in an animal's feeding trough instead of in the cradle he had lovingly made at home in Nazareth.

Once in Bethlehem, it seems that Joseph decided to stay there for a while. He found a house where he could live with Mary and the baby. But then Joseph had another dream and was warned by an angel to take Mary and the child and run away to Egypt.

They spent several years on the run from Herod before they eventually went back to Nazareth. By then Jeshuah was too big for the cot.

How did Joseph cope with it? Did God suddenly make him easy-going and flexible overnight? Or did he live for years with a growing sense of irritation at the unpredictable life God had forced on him? Was that the cause of his early death? By the time Joseph died, he and Mariam had two other sons, James and Jude and some daughters, too. Jeshuah, or Jesus, as we know him, took over the running of the family business.

Joseph had taught Jesus to measure to the nearest millimetre, to cut and shape the wood to exactly the right dimensions, to keep careful accounts. It was a good training for the next stage of his life.

When, eventually, he left his earthly father's workshop, he obediently went about his heavenly father's business with the same meticulous attention to his heavenly father's will.

Prayer

Heavenly Father, please help me to be meticulous in following your will and to have a careful attention to detail whenever it's appropriate. But please don't let me lose sight of the big picture and please help me to be flexible when you lead me in unexpected directions.

You can read about Joseph in the Bible in Matthew, chapters 1 and 2.

DAY FOUR

Snubbed

(Augustus and Quirinius)

Miles away from Nazareth, two political leaders went about the affairs of state, unaware of the birth of Jesus and oblivious to what was going on. Caesar Augustus in Rome, Quirinius, somewhere in Syria – possibly Damascus. Their sole part in the events surrounding Jesus' birth was to order the census which resulted in Joseph and Mary's journey to Bethlehem. Luke needn't have mentioned them, but he had a good reason to do so.

Just stop and think for a moment: what kind of a story is the nativity?

Every story has a *genre*. When we know the *genre* of a story, we know how to respond to it. Writers always glve clues which tell us what *genre* they are using and how they expect us to react. Let me give some examples: a story might be a tragedy, a romance, a thriller, an epic myth, or an item on the nine o' clock news.

You could present the Christmas story in many forms. Here are some suggestions:

The Hollywood nativity
A single-minded military veteran from the far north, now working as

a carpenter, wins through at all odds, protecting his teenage bride as their baby son turns out to be more than he seems and becomes the target of a vicious assassination plot.

The TV soap nativity

Good old Joe and Mary whom we all know and love and whose troubled romance we have followed with interest through several episodes, now have their child in unexpected, distressing and occasionally humourous circumstances, with a succession of bizarre and unexpected visitors.

The oriental legend nativity

A beautiful and innocent maiden attracts divine attention and, miraculously impregnated, produces a super-hero offspring, whom the evil, demonically inspired king tries to kill.

The pub quiz nativity

"Question: Which town, whose name means "house of bread", was the birthplace of the founder of one of the the world's major religions? And, for a bonus point, what was unusual about the baby's resting place? Answer: Bethlehem, birthplace of Jesus, and he was laid in an animal feeding trough."

Each of these approaches allows us some detachment from the story. They let us view it as something that happened far away and long ago, interesting and entertaining, but not really impacting on our lives today.

However, Luke's story doesn't fall into any of these categories. His approach is different again, and this is where Augustus and Quirinius come in:

> "In Rome today, Augustus Caesar… In Syria, Quirinius . . ."
> "Meanwhile, in Bethlehem, a city in Judaea, a remarkable birth took place."

Do you recognise the pattern? No? Let me update it to help you:

> "In Washington today, President Obama ... In London, Prime Minister Gordon Brown…
> Meanwhile, in the west bank city of Bethlehem, a remarkable birth took place . . ."

Do you recognise the style? You must do!. This is **the TV news nativity.**

When you watch today's news there will be mention of at least one great world leader – probably more. And you can bet that any baby mentioned will not be born to ordinary parents in a local maternity unit. Babies only feature in the news if they are born to famous parents, born miraculously, born in strange circumstances or are part of a royal family. Jesus, of course, was all of these. You will also know that a baby mentioned on the news is real. Story book babies appear in the soaps but not the news.

That's one of two reasons why Augustus and Quirinius figure in Luke's account of the nativity. They are there to tell us that this is not just an entertaining story – this is the news. The birth of this baby was an event of international significance with important implications for all Luke's readers – you included. Luke published the story, because it was "in the public interest".

This is a birth that makes a difference. The difference in the present is that your security no longer depends on Westminster, Brussels or Washington. The difference for the future is that you no longer have to answer to any Supreme Court on earth, national or international. Your security and your destiny now depend on the man who was born King of Kings in Bethlehem when Augustus Caesar was Emperor and Quirinius was Governor. In future it is to Him that you will be accountable.

The reference to Augustus and Quirinius also fixes the birth of Jesus as an event in time and space. It enables us to calculate to within a year or so the date of Jesus' birth. To get Augustus, Quirinius and Herod on the political stage at the same time gives us a window between 10 and 4BC. There would only have been one census during that period, and that was the one when Jesus was born.

The birth of Jesus had a date and a location. This is no fairy story – it really happened.

World rulers come and go. Augustus, Quirinius and Herod are long gone.

But the kingdom of God remains, still growing in power and influence.

Daniel saw it coming:

> "In my vision at night I looked,
> and there before me was one like a son of man,
> coming with the clouds of heaven.
> He approached the Ancient of Days and
> was led into his presence.
> He was given authority, glory and sovereign power;
> all peoples, nations and people of every language
> worshipped him.
> His dominion is an everlasting dominion that will not
> pass away,
> and his kingdom is one that will never be destroyed."
>
> – Daniel 7 v. 13 - 14

Caesar Augustus and Quirinius are referred to in the Bible in Luke, chapter 2, verse 1.

Prayer

Father, you have power to raise up rulers and to remove them. Thank you that you have established your son as king, that he reigns over all and his reign will never end. Let your kingdom come in my life and in your world today. In obedience to your word, I pray for all those in authority in the world, that we may have a peaceful and quiet life.

THE DATE OF JESUS' BIRTH

Augustus Caesar reigned as Emperor in Rome from 27BC to 14AD.

To begin with, Quirinius was a military official. He worked in Syria between 10 BC and 7 BC. In 6 BC he became Governor of Syria. Records show that he carried out a census in 6AD which provoked a rebellion. This may not have been the first census and, if the interval between one census and the next was ten years, there could well have been a previous one in 6 BC. The Jewish historian, Josephus, says that the census at the time of Jesus' birth was carried out under Saturninus, who was Governor of Syria between 9 and 6 BC.

King Herod, the other major political leader of the time, died in 4 BC. Jesus must therefore have been born between 6 BC when Quirinius took office and 4 BC when Herod died. Matthew 2 v 16 suggests that Jesus could have been born up to two years before Herod's order to kill the babies in Bethlehem.

Thus, the evidence points strongly to Jesus' birth occurring in 6 BC, with the census possibly starting under Saturninus' administration and then being completed while Quirinius was governor.

DAY FIVE

Counted in

(The Extras)

Every film has its "walk-on" parts, characters who are only incidentally involved in the plot and whose role is to stand around, make up a crowd, or be part of the background. The names of the "extras" don't get listed in the credits – they are anonymous, but without them the impact of the film would be greatly reduced.

I'd never thought about the walk-on roles in the Nativity until I attended a staff carol service in the County Council offices. A few days before Christmas each year the County Council held a brief carol service in the staff lounge at County Hall. A brass band from one of the schools played the carols, there was a talk from a visiting minister and a greeting from the Council Chairman who wished the gathered public servants a happy Christmas and reassured them that their work really was valued, even though budget restraints meant services would have to be curtailed once again and they would all need to work harder to achieve the same results with less resources next year.

There was a Bible reading which included the reference to the census, and it suddenly dawned on me that the word "census" was

very much at home in such company. In the event of a census many of the "human resources" standing around me would be either doing the counting, or making use of the figures in the course of their work.
My mind began to run away with the thought. I began to picture hundreds of long-forgotten local government officers, whose walk-on role in the Christmas story is never acknowledged. I imagined them organising the census, collecting statistics, setting budgets based on the census findings. Just like the local government officers around me, those people were struggling to carry out government decisions that stretched their resources.

My imagination ran wild as I warmed to the theme: harassed staff at the Bethlehem Tourist Information Centre finding accommodation for the flood of visitors; frantic librarians at Jerusalem City Library hunting down references to the Messiah's birthplace in response to a memo from the Palace; perhaps a social worker preparing a report on a homeless family living in a stable with a child at risk.

They didn't realise history was in the making. What would they have thought if they could have known about the people at County Hall, two thousand years later, doing the same kind of work as them and counting our days from the year they did theirs? None of them was aware of the importance

TAXES

The purpose of the census that Caesar Augustus ordered was to register people for taxation. The Romans had an elaborate system of taxes. Each farmer had to pay 12% of each harvest and every adult had to pay the equivalent of a day's wages every year.

Tax collection was farmed out to businessmen – the "publicans" referred to in the Authorised Version of the Bible. They were allowed to collect whatever they could over and above the taxes in order to cover their own expenses. This made them very unpopular.

of the baby. To them, Jesus was a small adjustment to the projection for Early Years' educational provision.

The strains of the last carol died away, and with my colleagues, I went back to my desk. But I had a new perspective. You never know when you're making history. You never really know who you are dealing with, or the full implications of what you do. For all you know, there may be an unseen dimension which gives cosmic importance to your humdrum routine today.

Jesus said "Inasmuch as you did it to the least of these brothers of mine, you did it to me." Somewhere in the midst of your routine today there may be a baby, a child, a man or a woman who represents Jesus. And He is watching to see how you respond.

Prayer

Father, help me to trust in the eternal importance of the mundane things I do today. Whatever I do, help me to do it for you. And when someone sent by you crosses my path, help me to see you in them and respond with the love and devotion you deserve.

The reference to the census is in the Bible in Luke, chapter 1, verse 1.

THE CHRISTMAS TREE

The practice of decorating a tree on Christmas Eve goes right back to the Middle Ages. The Old Testament lesson set for Christmas Eve in the lectionary was the story of Eve's temptation in the Garden of Eden. To illustrate this, the custom arose of bringing a tree into the church and decorating it with tempting goodies and attractive, shiny decorations.

St Boniface, a Celtic missionary who took the gospel into Germany, used the evergreen fir tree to teach people about eternal life.

Decorating the fir tree with lighted candles symbolised the light of the gospel. Queen Victoria's German consort, Prince Albert, introduced the practice of decorating the fir tree on Christmas Eve to Britain and from there it spread to the rest of the empire and to the United States.

The tree reminds us why Jesus came – to die as a sacrifice to atone for the sins of mankind. It reminds us of how he died – nailed to a "tree" (an upright piece of wood) and it reminds us also to be strong in resisting temptation and quick to confess and ask his forgiveness when we yield to it.

DAY SIX

Out of this World!

(The Shepherds)

This has to be the greatest UFO story ever – a tale with all the ingredients of a "Close Encounters" blockbuster.

Picture a rustic landscape. The sky is full of shimmering stars and the hillsides are full of bleating sheep. Shepherds are "ooh-ing" and "aaring" to one another as they sit talking around the embers of a camp fire. Then, without warning, the scene is lit up by an intense, blinding, white light.

The shepherds shield their eyes against it. Slowly their sight adjusts and they dimly discern the shape of a being of some kind – something alive, but not human.

An alien invasion – what else?

Then a voice booms out:

"Today, in David's Town, a child has been born who will rescue the human race. You will find the baby wrapped up and lying in a feeding trough."

BETHLEHEM

The name Bethlehem means “bread house”. The first reference to the town is in the book of Judges, where it is recorded as being the scene of a particularly horrific crime. Later, it was the birthplace of David, Israel’s greatest ever king.

The shepherds have scarcely begun to recover from this first shock, when another surprise makes them jump out of their skins for a second time. A sudden, loud, unearthly chord of music echoes over the hillside and the sky is filled with extra-terrestrial beings, singing in incredible, heart-string-tugging harmony.

Be honest, would you have believed their story? I dare say it was a matter for heated debate in local bars for years after. But, according to Luke’s account, their reaction was quite matter of fact:

“Let’s go to Bethlehem now and see this thing that has taken place, which the Lord has made known to us.”

How long did it take for them to reach agreement on that? How long did each of them try to carry on as if nothing had happened, afraid it was all a dream and he was the only one that had it? How long before they noticed each other’s shaking hands, sweating brows and impaired concentration, and one shaken shepherd’s attempt to tell what he thought he had seen and heard gave them all permission to say “it wasn’t just you, I saw it, too”? How long before they summoned up the courage to go to Bethlehem to check it out?

My guess is that Luke’s report skips over a lot of detail and that it took a good hour or so before they decided to head for Bethlehem to look for the baby.

But there’s a big question hanging over this account that is posed by every UFO story:

Why them?

If there are beings from outer space trying to contact us, why do they always pick on an obscure Midwestern farmer or a forklift truck driver from Daventry? Why do they never pick a politician or a university professor? Why do UFOs always land in fields and deserts? Why does one never land on the lawns of the White House or the gardens of Buckingham Palace?

And the same question hangs over the account of the shepherds. Their special encounter was not with beings from another galaxy, more from another dimension. But the question still needs answering:

Why them?

SHEPHERDS

Shepherds had a bad reputation at the time of Jesus' birth. They were considered unreliable, were not allowed to give testimony in the law courts and had a reputation for theft. Flocks were only supposed to be kept in the desert and a rabbinic rule stated that any animal found between Jerusalem and a spot near Bethlehem must be presumed to be a sacrificial victim. This makes it likely that these shepherds were breeding animals for use in the daily temple sacrifices.

You see, no-one else other than the shepherds received this official announcement of Jesus' birth. The wise men drew their own conclusions from the appearance of a star. King Herod heard about the birth second hand. Caesar Augustus, ruler of all the known world, was totally snubbed – until his death he remained ignorant of the future world ruler born in one of his far-flung provinces. Mary and Joseph got one angel each – and they were the parents. The shepherds, apparently, were the only people to hear the angel choir.

Why them?

To be honest, we don't know. People have made intelligent guesses. Perhaps it was something to do with Jesus being the Good Shepherd? A few years later he would tell a story about a shepherd who left ninety-nine sheep in the fold and went out looking for one who was lost. In the story the shepherd rejoiced more over that one sheep than all the obedient ones who hadn't played hookey. Was this a case of God going out looking for some lost shepherds, calling them back into the fold of faith?

Jesus was the descendant of David, the king who started out as a shepherd. Perhaps this was a special divine honour for the shepherds of Bethlehem in recognition of their important predecessor? It could be. But then Jesus was the Bread of Life and the name Bethlehem means "bakery". Why no angels singing to the Bethlehem bakers as they got up early to bake bread to feed the town's hungry citizens?

In part, this was a fulfilment of the words of Mary's song. God honoured these humble, working men with an angelic choir and snubbed the rich, famous and influential people in the land.

Some people have suggested that these were no ordinary shepherds. The lambs they were tending were destined for use as sacrifices in the temple, perhaps even in the annual Passover festival. Jesus was the Lamb of God who had come to take away the sin of the world. For Christians, he is the greater passover Lamb, the fulfilment of the Old Testament foreshadowing. Because of his death, we can escape our slavery to the law and its penalties and when God sees Jesus' blood applied by faith to believing Christians, he passes them over and ignores the guilt of their sin. Jesus came to make the temple and its sacrifices unnecessary and to replace the Passover.

That would make this angel choir the most elaborate redundancy notice ever given to any group of workers in history.

In the end, it probably comes down to grace. They weren't special, they weren't significant and for reasons known only to himself, God chose to let them hear the good news in this way. The reality is that none of us deserves to hear about the Saviour. None of us hears the gospel and gets the chance to respond to it because we are special, or significant, or "worth it". God lets us hear and lets us respond, because he chooses to. It's an undeserved favour. To use the theological jargon – a *grace*.

Of course, we're assuming the shepherds *were* the only people to receive an angelic announcement. Perhaps they weren't. Maybe there were scores of others: bakers, carpenters, builders, vinedressers, farmers, scribes, rabbis who also saw and heard the angels, but each of them put it down to eating too much cheese or drinking too much wine the night before. It could be that hundreds of people saw the angels but they all said: "No, I'm seeing things; that didn't happen" and went back to sleep.

Be that as it may, the really significant thing about the shepherds is their response. Once they got over the shock and took in the message, they immediately went to check it out.

- They went.
- They looked.
- They came back full of joy.

Simple faith. That's what God wants from all of us. For us to hear about Jesus, to check out for ourselves whether the gospel works and to discover the sheer joy of knowing Jesus and having our sins forgiven.

You can read about the shepherds in the Bible in Luke, chapter 2.

Prayer

Thank you Lord Jesus that, as the Lamb of God, you died in my place. Please be my shepherd today and help me to follow you in simple trust.

DAY SEVEN

At Last!
(Simeon)

The Old Year and the New Year. An old man and a baby. Past and Future.

Remove the scythe, and Simeon probably looked like Old Father Time. He was one of those elderly people who keep hanging on beyond their day, outliving all their contemporaries. His eyes still had a twinkle. His spirit was still full of strength, but his body was a wrinkled bag of bones held in life by the sheer power of his will. Simeon refused to die.

He refused to die, because there was something he was waiting for. Something God had promised him. Each day he went to the temple. Each day, he waited and prayed. Each day he went home disappointed – but determined to hang on.

Then, one afternoon, he shuffled into the temple courts and met a couple with a baby. The timing was perfect. They reached the entrance at the same time and walked in together with him. As they met, the Holy Spirit witnessed in his heart that this was it – the fulfilment of the promise God had given him decades before: "you will not die until you see the Lord's Anointed King".

Mary and Joseph had come up to the temple from Bethlehem to make the appropriate offerings for the end of Mary's confinement. The old man spoke to them, admired the baby, and gently took Jesus into his arms. He gazed into the little one's eyes. A broad smile spread across his toothless face as he turned his gaze upward and spoke:

> "Now, Almighty Ruler, you can release your slave in peace,
> according to your promise;
> For my eyes gave seen your rescue plan
> Which you have prepared before the eyes of all the people:
> A light of revelation to the gentiles
> And the glory of your people Israel!"

THE TEMPLE

The Temple in Jerusalem was still under construction when Mary and Joseph brought Jesus for this visit. It was the third temple to be built on the site. The original temple built by the emperor Solomon had been destroyed by the Babylonian emperor Nebuchadnezzar in 586BC. A second temple was built after the exile in Babylon by the Governor Zerubbabel and this was destroyed by the Roman general Pompey in 63BC. Herod began to build a new temple, starting in 19BC. The main structure of the building was finished in 9BC, but work continued until about 46AD. Every time during his life that Jesus revisited the temple, there would be something new to see.

"But how did you know?" Joseph asked in amazement. This was getting exciting; Mary's encounter with the angel – the miraculous conception – Joseph's dream – the shepherds with their story of the angels singing on the hillside, and now this. Eyes shining with excitement, they told Simeon the whole story so far.

Simeon returned the baby to Mary, lifted his frail hands, rested one on Mary's shoulder and one on Joseph's arm and blessed them.

"This child is going to cause the fall and the rise of many in Israel…" he said. Then he hesitated, made a little choking noise and with a tear running down his face, continued: "… and, my dear, your heart will be pierced through with sorrow. The thoughts of many hearts will be revealed."

For a while, Simeon savoured the moment. Other people came and joined him in admiring the baby. He watched as Mary and Joseph made their offerings. He walked back to the gate of the temple with them and waved them on their way. Then he shuffled home with a smile on his face.

The excitement had tired him out. He lay on his bed, went to sleep and died. When they found his body, the smile was still there.

Everything comes to those who wait, they say. Personally, I can't stand waiting. I want things to happen now. If not, I want to be doing something to make them happen soon. But sometimes, life just isn't like that. God has His moment, and we have to wait for its arrival.

Maybe there's something you have been waiting for. God promised it, you've kept asking for it. People have encouraged you to keep believing, keep trusting, but it hasn't happened. You've got impatient and impatience has spilt over into despair. The voice of the enemy is whispering in your ear:

"It's never going to happen."

Take courage from Simeon. Imitate his example. It happened. The moment came. He relished it and died a happy man.

Your moment will come too, and which way would you rather have it: elation now, and then a lifetime of anti-climax? or a lifetime of expectation with a moment of joy at the end?

There are pivotal moments in life when one age moves into another. Moments that are like going through a doorway. Moments when you leave things behind and reach forward for new things. This was one. The old man was full of the past – not just his own long life but the whole history of his people, right back to David, to Moses, to Abraham. So full of the past, yet in his hands, he held the future – a future which included salvation from sin, a worldwide church, centuries of religious wars and yet a new peace of mind for those like him who were prepared to embrace God's gift.

The New Year is a pivotal moment. You let go of the past with a mixture of gratitude and relief and you embrace the future with a mixture of hope and fear.

None of us knows what a year will bring. The fulfilment of hopes or sudden death, days of waiting or moments of rejoicing, painful suffering or jubilant exaltation. There's no way of knowing. Sometimes it feels as if we hold the future in our hands, as if we can shape it and make it ours. But then it grows up and scares us and reminds us we are not in control. The only security we have in the future is Jesus. And, like Simeon, we can embrace him. With Jesus, our future is secure, not just for a year, but forever.

Father, when your answer is not "yes" or "no" but "wait" please help me to be patient and to keep trusting you. Thank you for all the blessings you've given me in the year gone by. Please take my hand in yours and lead me securely into all you desire for me in the year to come.

You can read about Simeon in the Bible in Luke, chapter 2, verses 21–35

DAY EIGHT

God's House Guest
(Anna)

Christmas is a time for the young" – how often have you heard people say it? It's usually the complaint of older people who no longer have the opportunity to join in the frenzied excitement of present opening in families with young children.

I always feel sad when older people write off Christmas like that. Yes, children have a whale of a time anticipating Christmas, opening their presents and enjoying them. True, young people have their round of parties, kisses under the mistletoe and Christmas romances. But these aren't the essence of Christmas. The real meaning of Christmas is for everyone and everyone is part of it. I much prefer the attitude of an elderly West Indian pastor who spoke at a carol service I once attended. He assured the congregation:

"This Christmas is going to be your best ever!"

He went on to explain:

"The older you get, the better every Christmas ought to be! You know why? Because each year you got the experience of the last year to build on. If next Christmas isn't the best ever, it your own fault – you only got yourself to blame, because you ain't been learning from the experience of the past!"

Four elderly people have major parts in the Christmas story. Unfortunately, due to ageism and ignorance on the part of those who produce nativity plays, they are usually left out. We've already met three of them: Mary's cousins Zachariah and Elisabeth, and Simeon, who took Jesus in his arms when he was brought to the temple. The fourth is Anna. I always think it is delightful that, while God sent everyone else to find Jesus when he was born, he spared these two saintly senior citizens the journey. He didn't ask them to go to Jesus – he brought Jesus to them.

I imagine that Anna and Simeon knew each other. They both spent most of their time in the temple and were of a similar age. Was there perhaps a little spark of affection between them? If they had met years before when they were young, there might have been a romance. But they met, in the courts of the temple, when they were both old and set in their ways. Instead of the fire and passion of young love, they developed a mature, pure and deep friendship. In long, leisurely conversations, they shared their past and explored their common devotion to God.

I imagine they loved each other in a fond, yet respectful and totally holy way. They didn't live in each other's pockets, but they were there for each other, whenever they needed a friend.

While Simeon was talking with Mary and Joseph, I imagine Anna came along and because she was a friend of Simeon's she felt no embarrassment about butting in on the conversation. Especially when she saw her old friend holding a baby. This was obviously something she had to share.

Anna was 84. She was a widow. She had been a widow for most of her life. As a teenage bride, she had married with high hopes but after only seven years of marriage, her husband died, or was killed – the Bible doesn't say which. It seems possible that, in those seven years, Anna didn't have a child. If she had, her children would have taken care of her when she was old. She would have had a son or a daughter to live with. Life as a widow in those days was tough. There was no social security, no state benefits, no pensions. What there was, for those who had no-one to take care of them, was the temple.

You have to understand that the temple was more than a place of worship. It was God's house. If no-one else took you in, you were God's responsibility. The temple was a cross between a cathedral, an abattoir, a warehouse and a home for the elderly and disabled. Animals were brought to be slaughtered and roasted as they were offered to God, but the meat was available to be eaten by the priests and Levites and those they cared for. People brought their tithes to the temple -- not just money, but the firstfruits plus a tenth of their flocks and their harvests. These were stored, partly to feed the crowds at the pilgrim festivals when Jews from all over the world flocked to join in the celebrations, but also so that those who were poor could be fed from the temple store.

Anna started by coming every day to collect a ration of food. As time went on and she became more and more frail, it became pointless to go home. She ended up living in God's house, as God's guest. Mind you, she earned her keep. She began by sweeping and cleaning and helping in practical ways, but the more she listened to the rabbis teaching in the temple courts and the more she joined in the worship and prayer, the more she grew in godliness and wisdom. God filled her with His Spirit in a way that was unusual in those days and she began to see things and know things in a miraculous way. People found that she would often tell them the key to their problems. She seemed to have an uncanny insight into their thoughts and feelings and would sometimes tell them things that were going to happen ahead of time. As she developed a reputation, she earned the title of "prophetess" and people came to her more and more for help.

Jewish law had an important principle that evidence was only admissible in court if it was affirmed independently by at least two, or preferable three, people (see Deuteronomy 17 v. 6). It's a principle that is also useful in judging prophecy. If either Simeon or Anna had spoken about Jesus alone, without the other, it could have been ignored as the ramblings of a foolish old man or woman. But their agreement gave weight to what they were saying.
Anna reminds me of Psalm 84:

> "How lovely is the place you dwell, O Lord of hosts!
> My soul faints as it longs for the Lord's courts . . .
> ... Even the sparrow finds a home
> And the swallow a nest to lay her young
> By your altars, Lord of hosts, my King and God
> Happy are the people who live in your house
> Continually singing your praise."

The temple in Jerusalem is gone, apart from the "wailing wall" but in its place God has provided something new – the possibility of taking God's presence with us by continually worshipping him and being filled with His Spirit. We can't live in the temple like Anna, but we can live in God's presence. You can make a choice to live in God's presence today by constantly remembering Him and seeing everything in relation to Him.

Prayer

Father, you are always with me. Please help me to live in your presence moment by moment.

You can read about Anna in the Bible in Luke, chapter 2, verses 36–38.

DAY NINE

Star struck!
(The Wise Men)

I often think there is something odd about the arrival of the wise men – they give a "Monty Python" touch to the nativity. Their presence is incongruous – camel riders on a set where everyone else has a donkey – Asians in a Jewish village occupied by Romans – wealthy men surrounded by poverty and jabbering away in their oriental language while everyone else is speaking Greek. The biggest incongruity of all, though, is the way they come talking about astrology to people who believe the future is in the hands of God.

I sometimes have a flight of fancy in which, as they ride into Jerusalem, the wise men encounter an Evangelical Christian. The dialogue goes something like this:

LEADING WISE MAN:

> "Where is the child who has been born King of the Jews? For we observed his star in the east and . . ."

EVANGELICAL CHRISTIAN: (with a sharp intake of breath):

> "Let me stop you right there, sir. I need to warn you that astrology is a deception of the devil. All kinds of fortune telling are specifically forbidden in the Bible. Whatever it was you

saw, I advise you to ignore it – it is guaranteed to lead you astray. Have nothing more to do with it."

End of story. No frankincense, gold and myrrh. No slaughter of the innocents. No flight into Egypt. A few unfulfilled prophecies and a reduced range of Christmas cards. No three kings and shorter nativity plays.

THE WISE MEN

The wise men were "magi" – experts in astrology who probably came from Persia. In the Christian calendar, the twelve days of Christmas end with Epiphany, the day that celebrates their arrival in Bethlehem.

Matthew doesn't refer to the wise men as kings. The idea that they were kings comes from a passage in Isaiah 60 which has often been thought to predict their arrival:

> "Arise, shine, for thy light has come and the glory of the Lord is risen upon thee. For behold, darkness shall cover the earth and gross darkness the people, but the Lord shall arise upon thee and his glory shall be seen upon thee. And the gentiles shall come to thy light, and kings to the brightness of thy rising."

This passage in the King James translation is responsible for the assumption that the wise men were kings. The New Testament doesn't even specify that there were three of them. The assumption was made that there were three, because they brought three gifts.

The English historian, Bede (AD 735), gave them names: Balthasar, Melchior and Gaspar, but no-one knows whether he got this information from an accurate source.

Well, it didn't happen that way. But what are the wise men doing there?

The wise men are representative outsiders. Gentiles. Pagans. But they are also typical of millions of people all over the world who are looking for something they haven't found yet. You might even be one yourself. All round the globe people are trying to make sense of their lives – searching for reality, purpose and significance in a hundred and one different ways.

Astrology is a popular route, even today. Spiritualism (trying to contact the spirits of the dead) is another. Then there's feng-shui, yoga, reflexology and aromatherapy. Some people go for fitness and diet regimes, or football or motor racing. The more daring go for bunjee-jumping while the more timid take up cross-stitch. There's voluntary work, crime and drugs, fine wines and strong spirits, art and music. In fact there is no end to the different ways people use to bring some level of meaning into their lives: golf and surfing, DIY and travel, business and politics – the list goes on and on.

Each activity or interest is like a star that people follow, hoping, like the wise men, to find their dream at the end of the journey. Some are seeking happiness or excitement. Some are looking for fulfilment and meaning. Some want to prolong and improve their lives. Others are looking for a new and better world. Each person is following a "star" of some kind that they hope will lead them to it.

The wise men's star led them to a city, where they were shown a book. The book led them to the Baby and in the Baby their hopes and dreams were fulfilled. It's a journey millions have made since. A journey you can take too.

Whoever you are, I guarantee you will find what you are looking for in Jesus and the God He came to reveal. Jesus provides the greatest happiness and the most exciting and fulfilling life possible.

He can offer a life which is not only fulfilling and enjoyable now, but one which goes on beyond physical death. He alone can make this world a better place. The world is already better for his having been here and one day He will make it perfect. He is the source of healing and health and the answer to world peace. He won't only improve the life you're now living, he offers you a better one to follow it.

WHAT WAS THE STAR?

The Bible says that, when the wise men saw the star, it was in the sky towards the East. It doesn't imply that the star moved. They understood the star to have significance – to speak of a king who was to be born in Judaea. They went to Jerusalem to pay homage and there the priests sent them on to Bethlehem, because of a passage in the book of Micah which predicted the birth of a great Jewish ruler in that town. On the way to Bethlehem they saw the star again. It was now ahead of them and appeared to be over Bethlehem as they approached the city.

There have been several theories as to what the star was. There are two plausible suggestions:

One relates to the planet Jupiter. An hour before sunrise on 12 August, 3 BC, Jupiter rose in conjunction with Venus, so that the two planets looked like one blazing light in the sky. Then on 25 December, 2 BC, Jupiter was stationary in the Heavens and would have appeared to be over Bethlehem, viewed from Jerusalem. This theory is attractive, but unfortunately it does not fit the dates of the political figures referred to in Luke's gospel. These suggest a date about 6 BC for Jesus' birth.

The astronomer Johannes Kepler suggested that there may have been a conjunction of the planets Jupiter and Saturn in 7 BC. This would have given a very bright light and could have had astrological significance for the wise men. It would also fit with the dates of the political leaders mentioned in Luke's gospel.

Today, as then, the Spirit of God is at work, reaching out to meet people and to draw them from the particular "star" they have chosen to the Book that tells them about the Baby who became a man and lived and died to obtain for them all they long for. Whatever star you are following, your quest ends at a manger in Bethlehem over 2000 years ago where your Creator entered human history. Correction: it doesn't end there, it ends when you meet him through His Holy Spirit whenever you are ready to reach out to Him.

Jesus came to this world with a purpose. That purpose started with Him living on your behalf the perfect life you failed to live. It continued with Him dying in your place the death you deserve to die and then being raised to life again. By doing this, He made it possible for you to have what your heart desires above all else. Look beyond the star. Read the book. Find the Baby. Discover the man. Meet the God – and kneel down and give him the best you have. That's your destiny.

Having said that, I need to also warn you that there is a Deceiver at work. He tries to trap people in blind alleys and stop them finding Jesus. But when Christians start off by warning people about the Deceiver, it comes across as if we are being judgmental and condemning. Criticising someone's star is a sure way to get their backs up and put them on the wrong road.

So I don't want to knock anyone's star. Each star that people follow represents a hope or dream. We all need hopes and dreams. If I know what your dream is, I can usually point you to the place in the Bible where it says that what you are looking for is to be found in Jesus – and then I can set you on the road to the place where your hopes can be fulfilled.

You can read about the wise men in the Bible in Matthew, chapter 2.

Prayer

Almighty God, Creator and Lord of the circling Heavens, You who hold destinies in your hand, please grant your guidance to all who are travelling and all who seek for truth and life. Bring all their journeys to a joyful end.

DAY TEN

Threatened
(Herod)

Herod was a "control freak". Mind you, given his situation it was difficult for him to be anything else. Few rulers have held such a stressful and insecure position as he did.

Herod ruled one nation on behalf of another, but didn't belong to either. Officials of both nations viewed him with suspicion and there were plenty of people who wanted him out of office – or dead.

The Roman Emperor had given him the title "King of the Jews". This was a reward for two generations of loyalty in which his family had carefully cultivated the favour of the imperial rulers. Julius Caesar appointed Herod's father, Antipater, to the post of Governor of Judaea. Antipater was nether Jew nor Roman. He came from Idumaea, to the south and east of Judaea. Today, we would call him an Arab. This appointment was an astute move on the part of the Romans. If Antipater didn't satisfy their requirements they could remove him without the Jews getting upset, and if the Jews were unhappy with what he did, they could disown him and easily replace him with someone else. He was the "meat in the sandwich". He could only survive by watching his back, staying popular with both sides and making sure no-one got the chance to challenge him for power. You didn't disagree with the Romans, so turning the position down wasn't an option. Antipater did a reasonable job and then made sure Herod, his son, succeeded him as Governor of Judaea. Herod later became Governor of Galilee too. He knew which side his bread was buttered on and did everything in his power to keep the Romans happy. They were so impressed with the ruthless way he kept his two provinces under control, that they awarded him the title "King of the Jews".

Having secured the support of the Romans, Herod then faced another threat – that of a rebellion by the Jews. The Jews hadn't taken to him kindly at first but, to keep them sweet, Herod embarked on a huge and costly project to rebuild the Temple in Jerusalem. As Herod saw it, he had two options in life: Option One: to stay in control, be a success and stay alive. Option Two: to lose control, become a failure and be killed. Staying ahead in the game took a lot of care and effort. He had to watch his back all the while to make sure no-one had a hope of replacing him. His method of dealing with opposition was simple – eliminate it. Anyone who had any chance of being viewed as a successor to him met a sticky end. Unable to trust and control his queen, Mariamne, he even murdered her, and later, when her two sons realised what had happened, he had them assassinated as well.

As long as he was young and quick-witted, Herod could keep it going, but the time came when he got old and began, as they say, to "lose it". His ten politically motivated marriages had left him with 15 children, some of whom began plotting and jockeying for position in the hope of taking over from their father. The economy went into decline. Herod started to feel his age and feel very vulnerable.

And this is the point where the wise men arrived, innocently asking "where's the new prince?" Coldly, ruthlessly, Herod calculated his response. He was a past master now at dealing with political threats. First he got as much information as he could: "When did the star appear?" "Where is the most likely place for a claimant for the throne to be born?" Then he took his decision. A simple command to an army officer: "Go to Bethlehem. Kill any male child aged two and under". His conscience had been seared by years of ruthless political activity. He gave no thought to the bereaved families, to the terror and trauma his action would bring into the life of that community. His only thought was to keep in control.

Sometimes we face situations where the only way to stay ahead in the game is to play dirty – to become more and more ruthless and unprincipled in order to stay on top and keep things going our way. It happens in business and in politics and sometimes even in family life. At that point you have to make a difficult choice – to be human and retire, or to stay put and become a monster. It sounds an easy choice, but it isn't, because to give up takes courage. It looks like defeat. It feels like failure. Herod chose to stay on and become a monster.

History is strewn with people who took the same decision: Bonaparte, Hitler, Stalin, Ceaucescu, along with more recent figures in the Middle East and the Balkans. Alongside the big names are smaller ones: lesser known politicians, company directors, tyrannical teachers, cult leaders, mafia bosses and abusive parents – even church leaders. Not all have killed, but all have suppressed the truth or restricted other people's liberty to stay in control and keep things going their way.

The baby that Herod intended to kill escaped. Jesus survived to show the world a better way. "He emptied himself, taking the form of a servant." "He was oppressed and afflicted, yet he did not open his mouth." "He did not insist on his own way." Confident in God and His relationship with Him, Jesus refused to compete or to control. He even went to the cross, hanging under an ironic inscription given him by the Roman Governor which said: "The King of the Jews".

SANTA CLAUS

You can't imagine a greater contrast than that between Herod and Father Christmas. Father Christmas started life as Santa Claus (a corruption of "St Nicholas"). This 4th century saint was the bishop of the Myra in the south east of Asia Minor – know known as Turkey.

The details of Nicholas' life are unclear, but it seems certain that he anonymously gave a present to some children. One version of the story has him tramping the streets after dark on his own birthday, a sack on his back, leaving presents at the doors of homes where children lived. Another version, more likely to be true, involves three sisters from a poor family who could not afford a dowry and so could not get married. To save them turning to a life of prostitution, the good bishop threw three bags of gold through their open window late one night.

To celebrate St Nicholas' feast day, on 6 December, the practice grew up of surprising children with gifts that apparently appeared from nowhere – through a window, down a chimney, mysteriously appearing in shoes or stockings left by the fire or at the end of their beds. Because December 6 is near Christmas, this tradition then became tangled up in the Christmas Eve celebrations and confused with a German tradition of the *Weihnachtsmann* who also left gifts for children. The familiar figure with twinkling eyes dressed in scarlet with a white beard and rosy cheeks first appeared in an advertisement for Coca Cola and rapidly became the accepted way to represent "Father Christmas".

Santa Claus has no place in the real Christmas story, but he stands as an enduring symbol of generosity, compassion, mercy and concern for the weak and vulnerable – an embodiment of the love of God which Jesus came to show.

Sometime soon, perhaps today, you are going to have to make a choice: to stay in control at the expense of someone else's freedom, or to let go and trust God to bring things round – to vindicate you if you're right and everyone else is wrong. When that moment comes. you can take the first step to becoming like Herod or the first step to becoming like Jesus. Which will it be?

Prayer

Lord, Thank you that you are there to protect me. I don't need to cling to power or assert power over others because the one who has all power is my defender. Help me to choose the path of servanthood, following in your footsteps.

You can read about Herod in the Bible in Matthew, chapter 2.

DAY ELEVEN

Unconsolable

(The Mothers in Bethlehem)

Within hours of Herod's command, the streets of Bethlehem were awash with the blood of its babies, mingled with the tears of their distraught parents. Matthew sketches the heart-rending scene with a quotation from Jeremiah:

> "Rachel weeping for her children; she refuses to be comforted because they are no longer there."

Rachel's tears had fallen centuries before. To begin with, she cried tears of pain and jealousy. Rachel shared her husband, Jacob, with her older sister, Leah. Leah produced offspring with sickening regularity while Rachel remained infertile. Any woman who has had problems conceiving will be able to imagine the agonies of envy and rejection that Rachel felt.

Later, Rachel cried again over her firstborn, Joseph. The baby she longed for came. He grew up a handsome and intelligent young man. But then he was apparently mauled to death by a wild beast – though they only found his blood-stained clothing and not his body.

In time, Rachel had another son. It was a hard labour. She cried tears of exhaustion and pain as the labour dragged on. But eventually she held the little boy she had longed for in her arms. Weak from the effort and the loss of blood she named him Benjamin. And then she died. Jacob laid her to rest near a town called Ramah (as far to the north of Jerusalem as Bethlehem is to the south).

Centuries afterwards, Ramah became the collection point for Jewish prisoners being transported to Babylon after Nebuchadnezzar's invasion. Those who were unfit to travel – the babies, the sick and the elderly – were slaughtered there in cold blood. The town echoed with the cries of women who had lost everything, including in some cases both their children and their parents. In his prophecy Jeremiah imagines Rachel, the mother of the whole Jewish race, lifting her voice with theirs in a wail of grief and devastation.

Grief is intensely personal, yet we all experience it. None of us is ever alone in our grief, there is always someone who can say: "I know just how you feel!" And yet each grieving person is convinced that no-one else could possibly understand their very personal pain.

To lose a child is the cruellest loss of all, especially for a mother. We expect to lose our parents, but not to survive our children, let alone to have them snatched from us as soon as they are born. For a father, to lose a child is an indescribable, heart-numbing shock. For a mother, losing a child means entering a state where she feels permanently that her heart and stomach are being ripped out. There is no possibility of comfort. To accept comfort, to allow herself to forget her baby, even for a moment, would be to deny her love for her child. Everything in her physical and emotional make-up cries out for the child she should still be nurturing and caring for.

History is full of weeping mothers; mothers whose children were killed in action as soldiers, mown down by drunken drivers, overdosed on drugs, killed after sexual abuse by paedophiles. Mothers whose children died in hospital from incurable illnesses or in mysterious cot deaths at home. Then there are the mothers whose babies miscarried before they were born, those who were pressured into having an abortion, and those who gave their children up for adoption. Others weep because the child they loved has become a shame to them. And finally there are those who weep for the children they have never been able to have.

As they weep, each grieving mother feels a surge of envy towards any mother who still holds a baby. Some of the mothers in Bethlehem would have known of the young couple who left for Egypt just before the slaughter. They would have known that somewhere between Bethlehem and the Egyptian border one Bethlehem mother still held a living baby in her arms. How unfair that just one mother and child escaped the slaughter – that God blessed only one father with a warning dream. Even today, grieving mothers look with bitter eyes on the nativity scene, or the madonna and child in the Christmas cards, and ask: “why her? Why not me?”

In time, Mary came to share their pain. She stood at the foot of a cross and watched her son die a slow, cruel death. He was a grown man to everyone else, God and Man in reality, but to Mary he was, and always would be, her baby. As the soldier pushed the spear into Jesus’ side and the last drop of life drained out of him, she felt as if someone had pushed a sword into her own heart – just as Simeon predicted.

God doesn’t expect you to accept comfort, whoever you are and whatever your loss. You may be a man or a woman. You may have lost a child or a partner, a friend or a job. Your loss is unique and God respects your grief. He doesn’t ask you to pull yourself together or to be brave. He doesn’t tell you not to be angry or to dry your tears. He doesn’t seek to justify the unfairness or to help you get it inproportion. He doesn’t suggest things you could do to cope with your loss. He does offer you a place to cry and weep. He does offer you strength to work through the grief. And He guarantees that one day, in this life or the next, he will recompense you appropriately and adequately for what he has allowed you to be deprived of and he will avenge your loss.

I've watched the tears of a woman who had a miscarriage and seen her happy as at last she held another child in her arms. I've shared the tears of an apparently infertile woman and later seen the joy in her eyes as she passed her new baby to me to hold. I know of a mother who lost one child through illness and then fell pregnant with twins. I once had a letter from a mother whose lovely daughter committed suicide in the middle of her nursing training. She wrote a note in a Christmas card to tell me about the joy she was having with her son's new baby daughter who looked just like the daughter she had lost. Ahead of me in the world to come, I believe my mother already hugs my two brothers and my sister who died almost as soon as they were born.

There is no easy answer for those who ask "why me?" and God will never force consolation on those who could never accept it. But ultimately, He is just and He is good. That's why the man who wrote the Psalm could say with confidence: "weeping may last for the night. But joy comes with the morning."

Prayer

Lord, please comfort all who are grieving, especially those who mourn the loss of children. Hold them in your arms, give them courage to keep living and in due time, turn their sorrow into joy.

You can read about the in the mothers in Bethlehem in the Bible in Matthew, chapter 2 v 16–18.

DAY TWELVE

Brilliant!

(The Baby)

One of my favourite paintings is *The Adoration of the Infant Jesus* by Gherardo Della Notti.

In the picture, Joseph stands in the shadows, behind Mary and two children who are looking into the manger. The artist has captured perfectly a look I've seen many times on the faces of children when they see a baby for the first time. Their eyes are alight with wonder and excitement. The scene is so realistic and natural that you don't immediately notice anything unusual. But after a while, the penny drops. There is something strange about the source of the light in the picture. The shadows are not thrown by moonlight shining in through a window, and the glow which lights up the children's faces doesn't come from a lantern or a candle. The only source of light in the stable is the baby.

The painting is so realistic and the children's expressions so captivating, that with a cursory glance, you don't register the strangeness of a glowing infant. It's only when you take a more careful look that you notice. In a subtle way, the artist has made a theological statement. Several other painters of the period used the same convention, reflecting something Jesus said later, as a grown man, "I am the light of the world".

Jesus didn't really glow as a baby, or at any other time except for one strange incident when he was momentarily transformed in front of his disciples on the top of a mountain (see Mark, chapter 9). He didn't have one of those gold rings round his head, either. Jesus seemed like a normal baby. I imagine he cried when he was hungry. He made a fuss when he had wind. He needed to be fed and to have his nappies changed. He grasped onto a finger when it was put into his hand, he laughed and kicked when he heard Mary's voice. He slept a lot. Eventually he bit on everything he could find to help his teeth come through. He learned to crawl and talk just as any other baby does.

There is so much we would like to know about Jesus as a baby. How heavy was he? What colour were his hair and his eyes? Which members of his family did he resemble? Did he cry a lot? Did he take his feeds? The Bible is silent about all of this, but there is enough information to reassure us that Jesus was neither a religious

apparition or an alien from outer space. He entered the world as any ordinary baby would. Mind you, having said that, the words "ordinary" and "baby" hardly belong together. Other babies are ordinary in comparison to Jesus because of who He was and is, but you can never properly describe any baby as "ordinary". I've admired scores of new-born babies in my time and attended the birth of my own two children and none of them could be described as "ordinary". Each of them was extraordinary – totally unique.

I always think the most extraordinary thing about a baby is that you have no way of telling what it will become. Are you holding in your arms a future world leader? or a mass murderer? Will this little girl be another Marilyn Monroe or another Mother Theresa? Are you holding a car mechanic who will watch football every Saturday and do the best he can for his kids, or a scientist who will change the world through some amazing new discovery?

Mary and Joseph must have had a similar sense of wonder as they held Jesus. "He is the Messiah". That's what the angels and the prophets and an astrological sign told them. But they had never seen a Messiah before. They couldn't picture what it meant and they couldn't be sure what they had been told was right. Mary, Joseph, the shepherds, the wise men, Zachariah, Elizabeth, Simeon, Anna and whoever else saw the baby and held him in their arms – all they could do was look and wonder.

Looking back through history, we can fill in the details: how he ran off to talk to the scribes in the temple when he was twelve; how he turned water into wine at the wedding; how he healed people and how the demons reacted to him. We know about the Sermon on the Mount and the parables, about Gethsemane and the cross, about the resurrection and the Holy Spirit. We know about his billions of disciples, in every age and from every social class and language and nation, all with stories of answered prayers. To us he is no longer a baby. No longer even just a man.

For us He is the risen Lord, God made flesh, the rightful and future king of the whole human race – of the whole universe.
The Bible promises that one day every eye will see him. Until that day comes we can't literally gaze on him, "in the flesh" as they did.

But you can gaze on him by faith. You can read about him in the Bible. You can think about the things he said and did. You can draw near to him in prayer and experience His Spirit touching yours. And as you do, you'll be changed:

> "All of us, reflecting the radiance of the Lord with uncovered faces, are being transformed into his image, from one degree of radiance to another."
>
> – (2 Corinthians 3 v 18)

Come closer and look, but not down at a manger, because he's no longer there. Look into the Bible. Look through it by faith at His cross and His empty tomb. Look around at His followers and see his glory reflected in their lives. Look up to the clouds through which he promised to return and look still higher, to the throne from which he now hears and answers prayer.

Look, and see for yourself the change that looking brings.

Prayer

Light of the world, please penetrate each corner of my life. Drive darkness away and let the reflection of your radiance in me bring light to others.

You can read about the birth of Jesus in the Bible in Luke, chapter 2.

DAY THIRTEEN

Home for Christmas

(You and I)

I once spent the night before Christmas Eve in a house under the flight path out of London Heathrow, one of the world's busiest airports. It wasn't the best night's sleep I ever had! Because of the extra Christmas traffic, planes were taking off about every five minutes. Each time, the house shook as another airliner roared overhead, its engines straining to produce enough thrust to lift a full payload into the sky.

Every Christmas it's the same story – crowded airport terminals, extra coaches, trains with standing room only. Everyone wants to get home for Christmas. Bethlehem was like that the first Christmas Eve. Native Bethlehemites headed home from all over the Empire, creating congestion and confusion as they thronged into the little town for the census.

"Home for Christmas" – don't the very words tug at your heart? There is only one right place to spend Christmas day – in your own home, round your own table, with the people you know and love the best. Every year people struggle through fog and snow, wind and rain, enduring traffic jams and crowded public transport to achieve the dream.

Against the background of this stampede for home, John's statement about Jesus has a special pathos:

> "He came to his own place, and his own people did not receive him."
>
> – (John 1 v. 11)

Christmas was when God came home:

- – home, to the family of David which he had taken as his own.
- – home, to the nation of Israel which he had chosen as his inheritance.
- – home, to the human race which carried his image.
- – home, to the world he had created.

But his people didn't make him welcome.

Just imagine – coming home for Christmas to find the door shut in your face, no room for you, and a hostile reception. That was what the human race did to God.

This wasn't the black sheep of the family, returning in disgrace. This was the master of the house, coming to claim his place; the King, coming to claim his throne. The insult is almost too great to comprehend. God himself came home to face hostility from his creatures. Why?

To answer the question, we only need to look into our own hearts. How welcome is Jesus there? What kind of welcome does the Lord of Lords and King of Kings find in your home and in your heart?

Jesus was rejected and eventually crucified by the community he was born into. He is still rejected by many today. But the rejection isn't total. There were "ordinary people" who "heard him gladly" and disciples who gave up everything to follow him – though their imitation of Jesus was a long way from the reality. Some people received him then and some welcome him still. To those who did welcome Jesus, and those who welcome him today, John says:

> " . . . he gave [them] the right to become God's children."

When they come to the end of their time on this earth, those who have gained that right to be God's children look forward to a new home. Their home is no longer on this earth, but in Heaven, because Jesus said:

> " In my Father's house there are many rooms. If it were not so, would I have told you that I am going to get a place ready for you? And if I go to prepare a place for you, I will come back again to take you where I am, so that you can be with me."
>
> – (John 14 v. 1–3)

"Home is where the heart is", says the old proverb. But no matter how precious your home and your family circle, there can be a better belonging – a citizenship in Heaven – a special room in your Heavenly Father's house. In the words of an old American gospel song:

> "This world is not my home, I'm just a-passing through
> My treasures are laid up somewhere beyond the blue
> They're all expecting me and this one thing I know
> That I don't feel at home in this world any more."

Every Christmas there are people who are left out of the cosy family circles – people who find themselves alone and rootless because of circumstances and others who are alienated from their families. If that's you, you can have a sense of belonging – a home to look forward to in the life to come and a family to belong to here and now.

And if you are going to enjoy, or have enjoyed, this Christmas at home in the place you belong, with the people you belong with, remember: God doesn't want you to cling to it too tightly, because he has something better for you to look forward to. As one early Christian wrote:

> "Here we have no permanent city;
> we are looking for a city yet to come."
>
> – (Hebrews 13 v. 14).

Christmas at home with your family is just a sample – a foretaste – of something far, far better to come.

Prayer

The foxes found rest,
And the birds their nest,
In the shade of the cedar tree;
But thy couch was the sod,
Oh Thou Son of God,
In the deserts of Galilee.
O come to my heart, Lord Jesus;
There is room in my heart for Thee.

- Emily Elizabeth Steele Eliot
(Christmas carol)

This chapter is based on some words in the Bible in John, chapter 1, verses 10–14.

www.ingramcontent.com/pod-product-compliance
Ingram Content Group UK Ltd.
Pitfield, Milton Keynes, MK11 3LW, UK
UKHW020235250726
13967UKWH00001B/387